WHAT OTHERS ARE SAYING...

"Get Up & Grow is a book that is right for anyone who has chosen to move forward. Duke Matlock brings his experience of three decades of coaching people to Get Up & Grow. This book gives you step by step principles that will not only inspire you but will guide you into the next phase of your wonderful life."
Tim Storey, (timstorey.com)

"Every person hopes to be successful. But true success requires more than 'hope'. Get Up & Grow provides a clear daily plan that, if followed, will open the door to the extraordinary success that eludes the wanderers."
Dan Miller, Author and Coach (48days.com)

"Even champions need a coach. My good friend, Duke Matlock's book, Get Up and Grow, will help you employ the habits of successful people. Champions do daily what the average occasionally do. This book will help you win."
Neil Kennedy, Five Star Man

"Duke Matlock has written a fantastically practical book for leaders who are ready to take their life and vision to the next level! Get Up and Grow is a map for success and victory. The Bible says in Psalms 37:23, "The LORD directs the steps of the godly. He delights in every detail of their lives." This book will help you follow the plan that God has for you! This book is long overdue, especially for those like me who always had great passion, but needed to get the basics of discipline in place. I highly recommend this book!"

Patrick Schatzline, Evangelist and Author,
Remnant Ministries International

"Growing into the person you want to be (and that God designed you to be) is not easy, but it is possible. In the chapters of Duke's book, you'll find insight, advice and a doable plan for growth. Let Duke coach and encourage you toward success."

Chad Hall, President, Coach Approach Ministries

GET UP AND **GROW**

GET UP
— & —
GROW

21 HABITS OF SUCCESSFUL PEOPLE

DUKE MATLOCK

NEW YORK

NASHVILLE • MELBOURNE • VANCOUVER

GET UP AND **GROW**

21 HABITS OF SUCCESSFUL PEOPLE

Published in New York, New York, by Morgan James Publishing. Morgan James is a trademark of Morgan James, LLC. www.MorganJamesPublishing.com

The Morgan James Speakers Group can bring authors to your live event. For more information or to book an event visit The Morgan James Speakers Group at www.TheMorganJamesSpeakersGroup.com.

Scripture quotations are taken from the Holy Bible, New International Version, NIV. Copyright © 1973, 1978, 1983, 1984, 2011 by Biblica, Inc.TM Used by permission of Zondervan. All rights reserved worldwide. www.zondervan.com The NIV and New International Version are trademarks registered in the United States Patent and Trademark Office by Biblica Inc.TM

ISBN 9781683505914 paperback
ISBN 9781683505921 eBook
Library of Congress Control Number: 2017907732

Cover Design by:
McKenzie Matlock

Interior Design by:
Chris Treccani
www.3dogcreative.net

In an effort to support local communities, raise awareness and funds, Morgan James Publishing donates a percentage of all book sales for the life of each book to Habitat for Humanity Peninsula and Greater Williamsburg.

Get involved today! Visit
www.MorganJamesBuilds.com

*To Kelley, Jennifer, McKenzie, and Logan,
my greatest gifts.*

TABLE OF CONTENTS

FOREWORD

I learned from a very young age that if I wanted things to change in my life, I had to change what I was doing. As a teenager, I wanted a car. I very badly wanted transportation, and I wanted a vehicle that was my own.

Thinking about cars didn't help me get a car. I could think all day long about how great it would be to have a car and to be able to drive my friends around, but simply thinking about a car didn't produce a car for me. Looking at cars helped me decide which one I wanted, but I could look for weeks and it still wouldn't give me a car. Wishing didn't get me a car, either.

If I wanted a car, I needed to change something; so I changed what I did with my time. I got a job. Then, I developed a habit of saving the money I made from this job. Several months later, I was able to purchase my first car. The changes I made in my life resulted in the fulfillment of a dream.

I love seeing people make life changes in order to reach their goals, and I admire people who work hard to realize a dream. Duke Matlock inspires me. I met with Duke a year ago to discuss a coaching program of mutual interest—then we both got busy—and it was a year later before I had the chance to see

Duke again. When I did, I was amazed. In the intervening year, Duke had made changes to reach a goal, and his changes resulted in a 95-pound weight loss! Duke has personally traveled the road of setting goals, developing habits, and making changes. He shares his inspiring message in this book, Get Up and Grow.

Duke's message will challenge you, encourage you, and push you to embark on your own change journey. Your outcome will be up to you. The truth I learned as a teenager is still the same today: If you want changes in your life, you have to change what you are doing.

– Dr. Dave Martin, 'Your Success Coach' and author of 12 Traits of the Greats and Another Shot

ACKNOWLEDGEMENTS

There are so many people to thank when I consider how much time, effort, and energy went in to making this book come to life. To save us all from being here far too long, I'll just name a few.

My writing partner, Logan Matlock. Thank you for being the grammatical wizard I most certainly am not. You have a way of helping me get my ideas on paper that I truly do not believe anyone else could do.

McKenzie Matlock, you make Invest Leadership happen. Thank you for your commitment to my success. Also, you have some pretty mad cover art design skills.

I know without a doubt that I would not have been able to write this book without my clients. I know the Get Up & Grow process works because you had the courage to try it out! Thank you for allowing me to join you on your journey to success.

Finally, our Publisher, Morgan James. David Hancock, thank you for seeing the potential in this book and being willing to take a chance on us. You guys are the best!

INTRODUCTION

This book is about changing your life. At first glance, it is an outline of a morning routine made up of 21 habits. And while those habits are incredibly important, they are simply tools to be utilized on your journey to success and growth. The purpose of this book is not to add things to your to-do list; the purpose is to give you what you need to change your life. The habits, when implemented with intention and passion, give structure to your morning and discipline to your day.

There are a few ways to read this book. It can easily be read in one sitting while having a decent grasp on the concepts. I would recommend, however, that you read one habit every day for the next 21 days. Adopt one habit per day until you reach the end of the book. I also recommend that you download our free resources from dukematlock.com/downloadresources. These infographs and PDFs will help you as you read this book. Take your time as you read; lasting growth rarely happens overnight.

Striking Gold

A few years ago, my wife and I decided to plant a garden in our backyard. My wife loves gardening; she's always had flowers and small trees in our yard that she enjoys tending to. But for some reason, we had never tried our hand at a vegetable garden. So, we decided to utilize the resources we had at our disposal and put our land to good use. It was easy to see the potential laying beneath the surface; all we had to do to see results was dig a little deeper.

What would you do if you were planting a garden in your backyard and started digging up gold? How would you respond? I can assure you of one thing, if I struck gold in my backyard, I would keep on digging! I would call a land surveyor and have him come out quietly and take a look. I would probably buy out my neighbors and begin digging in their yards. I would do everything in my power, use every tool at my disposal, to exploit that resource.

Regrettably, I have yet to find gold in my backyard; in fact, the best things to come from my vegetable garden were the tomatoes. What I have discovered, however, is that within each and every person there is a well of untapped potential. There is the potential for greatness, for growth, for fulfillment, and for success. What most people lack is not the capacity, but the willingness to pursue and invest in discovering that greatness. There is a reservoir of untapped potential within you, as well.

My hope is that through reading this book, you will begin to tap into your potential. My prayer is that you will realize that *you* are your greatest resource. You are a suburban backyard filled with gold, just waiting to be discovered. You are the resource that needs to be exploited. You are capable of greatness—all you need to do is spend some time investing in yourself.

I have been following Jesus for nearly 40 years. In all of these years, my relationship with God has continually changed and shifted. I believe every new season of life is a new opportunity to get to know Jesus. My spiritual and devotional life is not a uniform checklist that never changes; in fact, it's quite the opposite. Just as in the other relationships in my life, my relationship with God is always changing and growing. The habits I will be laying out in this book come together to form an outline—to be fleshed out in your own way. As you implement each habit, be aware of the fact that some days you will spend more time on certain habits than others. I would encourage you to make these habits your own. True growth will only come when these habits become more than just a checklist. They must become a part of the way you relate to God.

Understanding that you are your greatest resource, new questions are raised; specifically, how should you go about tapping into your potential? And, how can you exploit yourself?

Growth Habits

One way to discover your potential is through the development of strong habits. One of the greatest pieces of advice I've ever received came to me when I was a young man. My boss at the time told me to get a little bit better every day; to set small goals that can be achieved in a short amount of time. The point of this exercise was not to change my whole life in a single day, but to make small, incremental changes over time. That piece of advice is one that I've followed throughout my career. In both my professional life and in my personal life, I have seen the incredible impact of getting a little bit better every day. It's hard to beat someone who is always progressing and growing.

Daily growth begins in your habits. The habits we develop in our lives determine our paradigm. Your paradigm is the pattern of your life. The ways in which you spend your time, the manner in which you prioritize, and the goals you set for yourself all contribute to that paradigm. Each of those things, however, are determined by your habits.

Before we go any further, let's define a habit. Dictionary. com says a habit is "an acquired behavior pattern regularly followed until it has become almost involuntary." Did you catch that? Habits are behavior patterns! Habits become the paradigms of our lives.

Additionally, habits are so integrated into our daily lives that they become involuntary. Have you ever left work and arrived at home with no memory of driving there? You obviously drove yourself, but you were able to make that drive without thinking about it because it's such a deeply ingrained habit. You can drive all the way home on auto-pilot simply because it's a habit in your life.

Now imagine that your drive home was serving to help you grow, develop, and become a better version of yourself every day. When you invest in developing good habits, that's exactly what you're doing. You begin to perform simple tasks that make you a better, stronger version of yourself. When you do them every day, your growth becomes an unavoidable consequence of those habits.

Transitioning Leaders

I have seen many leaders go through transition, and I have experienced transition myself. Times of transition are some of the most significant and influential moments in life. The manner in which we handle moving forward determines our success in the next season. I have noticed, however, that successful leaders prepare for transition long before opportunities arise. Your level of preparation will determine whether you're thriving or simply trying to keep your head above water. I believe there are three ways leaders typically handle transition. Take a moment to download our free resource on transitioning leaders from dukematlock.com/downloadresources and let's get into those reasons.

1. Successful leaders **grow** into what's next. These are leaders who have taken the time to prepare for any possible transition or change that may occur. They have spent time becoming the best they can be, and when the time comes, they thrive in their new destination. They're successful because they have put energy into investing in themselves and investing in success.

2. Some leaders **fall** into what's next. These are the leaders who find themselves moving into transition and are just barely getting by. They learn as they go and eventually ending up where they need to be; however, this growth

process delays and sometimes even reduces their level of success.

3. Sadly, many leaders **fail** into what's next. These are leaders who are so unprepared for a transition they're facing that they crumble under the pressure. They don't have the necessary skills to succeed because they didn't prepare ahead of time.

Investing in growth is the only way to make sure you're ready for the opportunities that will come your way. The balance of these pages will outline 21 habits that I have discovered lead to incredible growth. Twenty-one habits can seem like a lot, but remember that these are small, incremental changes. I'm not asking you to completely change your life in one sitting. I am asking, however, that you spend some time investing in yourself. Specifically, some of your time in the morning.

A FOUNDATIONAL HABIT
WAKE UP EARLY

*"Early to bed and early to rise makes a man healthy,
wealthy, and wise."*
– Benjamin Franklin
Early Rising: A Natural, Social, and Religious Duty

Daily Habit #1:
Take Advantage of the Morning

One of my close friends and coaching clients is an enterprise level sales leader for a large tech company. He leads a high impact team that acquires and services large corporate clients. He has an eye for talent and is skilled at both networking and team building. We were on the phone recently and I asked him, "What's the secret to choosing the right people? What are you looking for that no one knows you're interested in?" I wanted his secret sauce of team building… his key to identifying successful leaders. His response was simple: "I choose people who have a solid morning routine. I can teach someone how to sell our products and service our clients, but I don't have time teach someone how to be a personal success."

I find this to be true: Public success begins with private victory. The discipline you have in the morning will determine the success you have in life.

But why the morning? There really is no other time like the morning. I love it. The quiet, the stillness, and the peacefulness that is found first thing in the morning is unlike anything I have found at any other time. The early hours of the morning are when I'm the most productive; I believe they can become the same for you. There's an old saying that explains the army gets more done before nine o'clock in the morning than most people do all day; they do so because they take advantage of the early hours of the day. With this plan, you will too!

Your morning sets the tone for your entire day. It makes a difference in your ability to concentrate during the day, manage your stress levels, and the quality of your sleep. Early morning productivity is proven to be greater than that of late nights. According to a study done at the University of North Texas, students identifying as early risers had, on average, a grade point average that was an entire point higher than their counterparts who identified as night owls. In fact, there is a greater level of rest that is found when the hours leading up to sleep are set aside for recreation and relaxation. To download a free resource explaining why the mornings are so important, head over to www.dukematlock.com/downloadresources.

One of the most beneficial elements the morning can offer is a time free from distractions. I like to wake up early enough to spend my mornings alone; I find that I am typically the only person awake in my home when I get up in the morning. I love my family, but when we are all moving around the house at the same time, I am unable to focus on investing in myself. I want to talk to my wife and spend time with my daughters when we're all awake. My early mornings allow for a time of personal investment that is uninhibited by distractions. When I am not distracted, I can optimize those early hours.

There is nothing selfish about investing in yourself. If you find you're feeling guilty about setting aside this time, remember that your relationships and your professional life become stronger when you become a better version of yourself. There's nothing wrong with investing in personal growth—my mornings belong to me, and me alone.

The time you get up in the morning will determine the pace and tone of the rest of your day. When you wake up early, you set priorities. You decide what parts of your life deserve attention and focus. You create space for growth. But if we're all being honest, waking up early can be difficult! Your bed will never seem as inviting and comfortable as it does when it's time to leave it.

The most important thing when developing a new habit like this one is consistency. I would urge you to try this for at least 21 days. Spend the next 21 days dedicating your mornings to personal growth. Truth be told, the morning is so important... I've found that if I don't act on these habits in the morning, I won't do so during the day. I will be too busy investing in other things to invest in myself. It won't take long before you see just how much mornings matter, too.

Waking up early is the first habit for a reason. These 21 habits come together to form a solid morning routine. They will be most effective and produce the most growth if implemented early in the morning. But before you can do that, you have got to master your morning. Get up early and you create the space for incredible growth.

Be Inspired:

"And rising very early in the morning, while it was still dark, he departed and went out to a desolate place, and there he prayed."
Mark 1:35

This verse shows us that even Jesus had a morning routine! The early morning was one of the only times that Jesus was able to be alone, pray, and focus on his mission. If the morning was that important to Jesus, it should be important to you and me as well.

Get Coached:

How can you utilize your mornings as a time of growth?

Take Action:

Set an alarm to get up early tomorrow morning. When it goes off in the morning, don't press snooze; get out of bed!

SPIRITUAL HABITS

INVEST IN SPIRITUALITY

We will focus on four areas of growth, starting with spirituality. There are very few things in your life that have an impact quite as great as your spiritual life. Before you can experience success, professionally or in your relationships, you must first discover wholeness and healing internally; once you understand this, your spiritual life changes. Your spirituality is about more than what you want to accomplish or how you want to grow; it's about who you are. Your spiritual life will determine your character, your perspective, and the way you relate to the world. Before moving on, you must first understand the value of feeding your spirit.

Once the importance of your spirituality has been fully grasped, it's time to take the steps to grow in this area. The next five habits will address five different ways to do just that. Keep in mind that we are looking to implement habits, not check items off a to-do list. Habits have the ability to shape your life; they are a part of who you are and the way you order your life. Spiritual habits make your spirituality an interactive relationship instead of a guilt-ridden checklist. This isn't about guilt... this is about growth. These five habits have the ability to transform your spiritual walk. I encourage you to participate actively in the steps we will be walking through and implement these habits over the next few days. The effectiveness of this process will be a direct result of the amount of effort you put into it.

SPIRITUAL HABITS
FINDING A VIRTUAL MENTOR

"Mentorship is simply learning from the mistakes and mastery of a successful person in his/her field."
-Bernard Kelvin Clive, *(attrib.)*

Daily Habit #2:
Listen to the Voice of a Spiritual Mentor

As I endeavor to grow, diversity of thought is of vital importance. Without the presence of other voices in our lives, our thoughts feed on themselves. Unchecked, thoughts can quickly form unhealthy alliances with one another; you only hear things from one perspective, and that perspective is yours! It's easy to see a lack of balance in your life and your decision-making process when you're not entertaining the influence of others.

One way I like to open myself up to influential relationships is seeking out mentors. Some mentors are in your life for years; they are driven by a personal relationship. Other mentors, like the ones I'm talking about, you may never meet. They are simply a voice, not a physical presence. A virtual mentor is that kind of voice. Virtual mentors offer a quick, concise nugget of wisdom and truth every day. They can even be delivered to you electronically.

Virtual mentors change often. Currently, I'm reading Rich Wilkerson. Rich writes a short devotional, called a SOAP, and delivers it to subscribers every morning. This devotional takes about 90 seconds to read. It is a clear, concise message that allows me to gain a fresh understanding of a passage of Scripture. Always learning something new, I allow myself to see the world for a moment from his perspective

Spiritually, you need to allow yourself to be molded and inspired by trusted sources. A blog subscription or daily email blast are tools that connect you with a virtual mentor. When you're looking for a spiritual mentor, find an influencer who can meet key characteristics to produce the best results. Here is a simple checklist you could follow:

- Someone you respect
- Consistently delivered content
- Content delivered directly to you
- Free
- Concise

Be Inspired:

"Therefore encourage one another and build each other up, just as in fact you are doing."
1 Thessalonians 5:11

Encouragement and influence are not just nice ideas—they are Biblical mandates. We cannot become the best versions of ourselves alone; we are made better by the voices of other people in our lives.

Get Coached:

Who is speaking into your life? How are these voices helping you invest in yourself?

Take Action:

Take some time today to do some research and find a virtual spiritual mentor. Sign up for at least one blog or website subscription that will help you invest in your spirituality.

SPIRITUAL HABITS
DAILY READING PLAN

"The Bible is the cradle wherein Christ is laid."
- **Martin Luther,** *Watchwords for the Warfare of Life*

Daily Habit #3:
Read from a Daily Bible Reading Plan

This time in your morning is going to become what many Christians would call your "daily devotions." I have been a Christian for a long time. Over the years, I have tried to find different ways to spend time with Jesus and become more like Him. No matter what I've tried or the different ways I've structured the time I have spent with the Lord, there's one thing of vital importance: reading my Bible.

In *Comeback & Beyond*, Tim Storey says, "God is big. Fill up with His principles for life and His dreams for your life. Believe them in your heart, speak them in faith, and take the first step of faith He tells you to take." The only way to make sure we're staying in constant communion with God, continually getting to know God, and becoming more like Jesus is to be in the

Word! We have to read, study, and meditate on the Word of God every day.

Sometimes this can be harder than it seems. The Bible is a long book! Maybe you feel overwhelmed, unsure of where to begin reading. Others of you may have already read through the Bible, heard many sermons on the same passages, or find yourself reading the same books and verses over and over again. This is where a daily reading plan comes into play. A structured plan provides accountability and takes all the guess work out of reading your Bible.

Maybe you need a structured plan to give you the ability to read through the entire Bible in a year. Maybe you are looking for a topical reading plan to help you work through a particular issue in your life. Regardless of the specific plan, the important thing is to find one that works for you and stick to it. Allowing the Bible to become one of the major voices in your life is incredibly important to your spiritual development and the only way to accomplish this is to read it every day.

Take a moment to write down what you are looking for in a daily reading plan. For example, do you want a topical plan or a 3-7 day plan? Be sure to write down what you're looking for; we'll use this list later on.

Be Inspired:

"For the word of God is alive and active. Sharper than any double-edged sword, it penetrates even to dividing

soul and spirit, joints and marrow; it judges the
thoughts and attitudes of the heart."
Hebrews 4:12

Read that verse again just to make sure you catch what the author is saying. The Word of God is truly a powerful thing! In reading Scripture, we are being molded and crafted to be more like Jesus. Isn't that the goal of every Christian? If that isn't our goal, then we've missed the whole point.

Get Coached:

How has God's word impacted your life in the past? In what areas of your life are you presently looking for God's direction? Where will you go to gain that influence?

Take Action:

If you haven't done so already, download a Bible reading app on your smartphone. Many of these apps include free reading plans. Using the list you made earlier, find a plan that works for you and start reading.

SPIRITUAL HABITS
READ

"A mind needs books like a sword needs a whetstone."
- Tyron Lannister, *Game of Thrones*

Daily Habit #4:
Read One Chapter from a Book on Spiritual Development

Books have the power to change your perspective, give you a fresh idea, or ignite a passion for something that you had never considered. The most successful and innovative people I know are avid readers. It is, without exception, a common denominator among successful individuals, regardless of industry or trade. I've discovered that the more I read, the more I want to… it really is life changing.

As a young man, I was told many times to continue growing and developing, I needed to learn to love reading. This is true in my spiritual life and in my professional life. Reading one chapter a day breaks your book down into bite-sized chapters, making it easier to follow and less overwhelming to digest. If you read one chapter a day, you will end up reading anywhere between 18-20 books in a year! That growth is worth investing in.

Books truly do have the power to change your life. Reading within the context of your spiritual life is no different. We live in a society in which incredible pastors, theologians, and leaders are able to write and publish books that we can easily access. We live in an exciting time that allows you to not only learn and grow from the wisdom of your pastor, but also from incredible leaders all over the country! It's an amazing thing.

Keep in mind that you'll be reading a variety of books, so be careful not to get bogged down trying to find the "right" one. Read authors you already know and love. Become confident in reading works from people you have yet to experience. Growth will come regardless of the book; just take the good, leave the bad, and keep reading. Guard your heart, but be willing to allow your worldview to be expanded by what you are reading.

Unsure of where to start? Here are a few of my personal favorites:

- *Circle Maker* by Mark Batterson
- *Divine Mentor* by Wayne Cordero
- *Jesus Is* by Judah Smith
- *21 Seconds to Change Your World* by Dr. Mark Rutland

Be Inspired:

"Observe them carefully, for this will show your wisdom and understanding to the nations, who

will hear about all these decrees and say, 'Surely this
great nation is a wise and understanding people.'"
Deuteronomy 4:6.

This verse is talking about the Israelites' desire to learn the law and adopt the principles of what they had been taught. Your ability to learn and grow from the wisdom and teaching of others is a sign of wisdom and understanding! That wisdom will become your calling card.

Get Coached:

What is the one book, other than the Bible, that has helped you grow spiritually? What about it made it so helpful?

Take Action:

With your answer to the questions above, look for a book with some of the characteristics you mentioned. Go on Amazon and read some reviews, or ask a trusted friend for reading suggestions. Find a book that will help you feed your spirit.

SPIRITUAL HABITS
REFLECT AND PRAY

*"To be a Christian without prayer is no more possible
than to be alive without breathing."*
- **Martin Luther,** *The Communion of the Christian with God*

Daily Habit #5:
Spend Time Reflecting on what You are Learning

There are few things in my life as valuable and powerful as prayer. At this point in your morning, you have heard from others and allowed yourself to be influenced by the voices of your mentors. You have read from your daily reading plan and have spent time reading a chapter of a book that fosters growth in your spiritual life. These things are vital to your growth, but you need to give yourself a chance to digest and think about the information you have just heard and read.

The first way to do this is to spend time in reflection. The early church and ancient Christian mystics believed in the power of meditation, as well as spending time in silence and solitude. There is something significant about taking the time to think and reflect quietly. It's in the silence we receive guidance and hear from God.

The second part of this habit is to pray. While reflection is a form of prayer, I make a distinction between the two because where reflection is an exercise in silence; prayer is a conversation. Prayer is a chance to talk to your Creator. Bring your concerns, your joys, your wins, and your losses before the Lord. Talking to God in this way has the ability to shift your perspective in ways that few other things can.

Spending time in reflection and prayer is so important in the life of every believer. You cannot hope to become more like Jesus or gain a greater understanding of who He is if you're not speaking with Him. When you pray, you submit your cause to Christ. You invite Him on your journey.

What are you praying for today? What are you grateful for? What areas are you struggling with?

Be Inspired:

"Do not be anxious about anything, but in every situation, by prayer and petition, with thanksgiving, present your requests to God."
Philippians 4:6

When you pray, anxiety and fear leave. It's difficult to be fearful of anything when you spend time in the morning talking with the Creator of everything.

Get Coached:

What are you praying about right now? How can you get the most out of this time in your morning?

Take Action:

Target the areas in your life that need prayer today. Bring your requests to God.

SPIRITUAL HABITS JOURNAL

"Ideas are the most fragile things in the world, and if you do not write them down, they will be lost forever."
-Phil Cooke, *One Big Thing: Discovering What You Were Born to Do*

Daily Habit #6:
Create a Record of your Spiritual Investment

When I introduce the idea of journaling as a way of investing in spirituality, I often experience resistance. But believe me, whether you are a writer or not, journaling is the absolute best way to close out this part of your morning. There's nothing that will allow you to collect your thoughts, keep a record of what you're learning, or set spiritual goals the way that journaling will.

In college, I was a bit of a shutter bug. I remember having a camera that seemed to be an extension of my arm. These were the days before cameras were technologically advanced enough to have an automatic focus feature. As a result, when I would go to take a picture, I would need to line up my shot, taking time to focus the lens before I could capture the moment. Not taking the time to focus the lens properly, my picture would be blurry and out of focus.

Journaling presents the opportunity to see a sharper image of what has taken place in your spiritual investment instead of seeing a collection of seemingly disjointed occurrences. Journaling brings focus and clarity to your spiritual investment, all while adjusting your perspective. When you write out what you've learned, you're able to see the big picture in a way that would have been otherwise impossible. Much more remains to be learned and gleaned as you step towards your spiritual investment. Journaling brings all of those this to the forefront, capturing a clear snapshot of what you've learned.

Remember, journaling can be whatever you want it to be. Whether your mind works in bullet points or paragraphs… you can journal. The goal of this exercise isn't to write a novel, but to create a record of your spiritual investment and growth.

Be Inspired:

"But Mary treasured up all these things and pondered them in her heart."
Luke 2:19

After the birth of Jesus and all of the miraculous events that followed, the Bible tells us that Mary spent time thinking and reflecting on the events which had taken place. One of the best ways to think, reflect, and remember is to journal. Spend time pondering what God is doing in your life and write them down. These records can encourage you, bringing to remembrance the faithfulness of God.

Get Coached:

How would recording your thoughts today impact your decisions in the future?

Take Action:

Set aside time this morning to journal. Write down what you learned today, the things you are praying for, and the spiritual goals you are setting for yourself.

SUCCESS HABITS

INVEST IN SUCCESS

I have spent the last 30 years in pastoral ministry. Something interesting I noticed during that time was many Christians have a hard time talking about professional success. Many people feel as though they must continually fly under the radar or live in obscurity to please God. This mentality is absurd. Believe God created you with the ability to lead and be successful. He designed you with talents and skills necessary to accomplish goals and be productive. When we invest in success, we are honoring God by cultivating the gifts and talents we were created with. God has called everyone to work and to work with excellence.

To invest in success is to develop habits that will grow who you are as a person before growing who you are as a professional. The habits we will be discussing over the next few chapters will walk you through that process. Your desire to develop must be combined with actionable steps if true growth is to take place, so let me encourage you to lean in to this process. Allow these habits to shape and mold how you understand of yourself. Remember, your definition of success cannot be determined by those around you; you must decide what success will look like in your own life.

Take a few minutes before you get into the habits to answer that question. What does success mean to you? What do you want to accomplish by implementing these habits, and investing in success?

The only things limiting your success are your leadership capacity and your daily habits. When you utilize your mornings as growth opportunities, you increase your capacity and develop strong, beneficial habits. So, ask yourself: Are you going to conquer your day or is your day going to conquer you? I'll tell you one thing; it's hard to beat someone who is always getting better. When you invest in success, you're investing in growth. Let's get started.

SUCCESS HABITS
VIRTUAL MENTOR

"Most people can do awe inspiring things. Sometimes they just need a little nudge."
- Timothy Ferriss, *The 4-Hour Work Week*

Daily Habit #7:
Listen to the Voice of a Success Mentor

In going through this morning routine, I believe you will gain an understanding of how important it is to have mentors and influencers speak into your life. Already we've discussed the process of finding a spiritual mentor, but your success mentor should be a new voice altogether. Not only do you need someone to speak into your life spiritually, you also need someone who will encourage and challenge your professional life.

Success mentors are vital. While you can learn an incredible amount from your colleagues and leaders, it's important to also find an impartial voice. A virtual success mentor is powerful because the relationship is not influenced by emotions or personal biases. A virtual success mentor will be a specific, focused voice that will help you grow.

Your success faces the same risks as your spirituality if you aren't investing in mentoring relationships. If you don't have a mentor, you are unable to utilize the experiences and wisdom of experts in the business world. Regardless of your profession, you can learn from people who have achieved success in their fields. More often than not, the principles of successful people can be applied to every person regardless of their profession.

I currently subscribe to DarrenDaily. Darren Hardy produces three-minute videos and audio files that are emailed or texted directly to his subscribers, each explaining a characteristic or principle of success. His videos are thought provoking and usually include a practical way to apply the principle. I also currently subscribe to Dr. Dave Martin and have in the past subscribed to Zig Ziglar, John Maxwell, Jim Rohn, and many others. Success mentors have life cycles in how they deliver their content; the success mentor you have today may not be the person you have tomorrow, and that's okay. When you reach the end of the life cycle with your success mentor, don't worry… just find someone else to invest in your success.

The same characteristics that you looked for in a spiritual mentor also apply to your success mentor. Let's refresh ourselves on that list. Utilize this checklist as you look for your success mentor.

- Someone you respect
- Consistently delivered content
- Content delivered directly to you

- Free
- Concise

Be Inspired:

"Moses' father-in-law replied, 'What you are doing is not good. You and these people who come to you will only wear yourselves out. The work is too heavy for you; you cannot handle it alone. Listen now to me and I will give you some advice, and may God be with you.'"
Exodus 18:17-19a

When Moses began leading the Israelites, he was in way over his head. He needed time to grow into his new role. It's clear from reading the story of Moses, however, that he would not have been one of the greatest leaders in the history of Israel had he not been blessed with the counsel of his father-in-law. Do you have a Jethro in your life? If so, make certain you're ready to listen.

Get Coached:

What role does mentorship play in your life?

Take Action:

Do some research today on success mentors. Look at the success blogs you read and see if they offer some sort of mailing list.

SUCCESS HABITS
READ

"Reading is to the mind what exercise is to the body."
- Joseph Addison, *Tatler*

Daily Habit #8:
Read One Chapter from a Book on Success

As we have discussed in an earlier chapter, not much else can maximize your growth and development like reading. Nothing challenges your mind, shifts your perspective, or broadens your worldview quite like investing in reading. Looking at the lives of highly successful people,

they all have at least one thing in common: They're readers! On your journey to growth and becoming better, your commitment to read is a game changer.

We discussed reading a book on spiritual development as a component of investing in your spirituality, but there's more reading to be added to your morning routine. Now is the time to select a book on success and leadership development.

Reading at least one chapter per day from this kind of book will have an incredible impact. It's important to read from a variety of genres and subject matters because there are different categories to your life. You have to feed what you want to grow; each area of your life deserves attention.

When you read about success and professional development, you allow yourself to learn from the experiences of others who have already attained success. You can learn from both their mistakes and their triumphs, reaping the benefits of their years of experimenting to find what works.

Choosing what to read is important, but let me encourage you not to overthink it. Read everything you can get your hands on—taking the good out of it and leaving the bad. You may find yourself reading books that you don't agree with, and that's okay too. One of the incredible things about reading is that, often, in reading the voices of others, you find your own voice.

Be Inspired:

"Then the Spirit came on Amasai, chief of the Thirty, and he said: 'We are yours, David! We are with you, son of Jesse! Success, success to you, and success to those who help you, for your God will help you.' So David received them and made them leaders of his raiding bands." 1
Chronicles 12:18

In this passage, the Spirit of the Lord falls on Amasai and he is able to encourage David. This encouragement not only solidified Amasai's relationship with David, but also contributed to David's success. Sometimes you just need someone to tell you that they are with you, believe in you, and trust in your ability to succeed. When you read, you receive that kind of encouragement!

Get Coached:

How has reading impacted your success and professional development in the past? What made that reading so impactful?

Take Action:

Pull a book off of your shelf or head over to Amazon and download one to your Kindle and start reading. Read one chapter from a book that will help you become more successful.

SUCCESS HABITS
BE GRATEFUL

"There are two ways to live your life. One as though nothing is a miracle. The other is as though everything is a miracle."
- Albert Einstein, *(attrib.)*

Daily Habit #9:
Write a Daily Gratitude

Self-deprecating thoughts are like weeds; they have no value and yet possess the ability to take completely over. Negativity is one of the most common agents of destruction when dealing with growth, success, and progress. Sometimes we are pessimistic about our circumstances; maybe we feel stuck or trapped. Other times, we are negative about ourselves. Defeatist self-talk can make us believe that we will never be good enough to accomplish our goals.

One of the best ways to overcome negativity is through gratitude. Gratitude plays a crucial role in the way you see the world. If you operate without gratitude, you will always feel like there is not enough to go around or that your relationships are somehow insufficient. This kind of negativity is the enemy of growth. True growth cannot come from a lack mentality—that kind of desperation will make you sloppy and disorganized. True growth comes from appreciating and using all of your resources to your advantage.

Whatever you water will grow. If you feed your negative thoughts, they will grow. When you cultivate an attitude of gratitude, however, you will fill your mind with positivity. When your mind is filled with grateful, hopeful thoughts, you will find there is no room for self-doubt, negativity, or a lack mentality.

To cultivate this attitude of gratitude, it has to become a habit in your life. As a part of your morning routine, write down at least one thing you are grateful for. This is part of your investment in success; because without gratitude, greatness becomes an impossibility. When you can call out the good in your own life, you can call out the best in others as well.

Maybe you don't feel like you have much to be grateful for. I would argue that you do. To help you get started, I've created a list below of a few things anyone can be grateful for. It's up to you to finish it.

1. Be grateful for the encouragers in your life.
2. Be grateful for the journey you are on.
3. Be grateful for family and friends.
4. Be grateful for small victories.

Be Inspired:

"Let the message of Christ dwell among you richly as
you teach and admonish one another with all wisdom
through psalms, hymns, and songs from the Spirit,
singing to God with gratitude in your hearts."
Colossians 3:16

Gratitude is an act of worship. When we express gratitude, we are thanking God for all that He has given and supplied for us in our lives. Gratitude is recognition of God's provision.

Get Coached:

What are you grateful for? How can you express this gratitude?

Take Action:

Grateful for the encouragers in your life? Take time today to pay it forward and encourage someone else. If you are grateful for your family and friends, let them know. Gratitude is contagious; share how you're feeling with the important people in your life.

SUCCESS HABITS
REVIEW YOUR AGENDA

"The secret of your success is determined by your daily agenda."
- John C. Maxwell, *Make Today Count*

Daily Habit #10:
Review what Your Day will Hold

Now that you've read, heard from your mentor, and expressed gratitude for the things in your life, it's time to look ahead. The day lies before you, and there are things that need to be accomplished. Each item should be on your agenda. Having a clear, specific task list will allow you to prepare for what your day will hold. Your agenda is more than a checklist. It's a game plan.

This is your opportunity to pull out your daily goals and look at what lies before you. It's very difficult to execute a plan or accomplish a task if you don't know exactly what you're looking to accomplish.

This is part of your morning routine because the start of your day sets the tone for everything that follows. Reviewing your task list at this point in your morning will enable you to walk into your office prepared and ready to work; you won't waste any time trying to get ready for your day once you arrive.

Preparation eliminates hesitation. When you are prepared, you set yourself up for success. Nothing combats fear or an indecisive attitude like feeling prepared. The best way to prepare yourself for what the day will hold is to review your agenda. Things may change throughout the day, but your foundation will be solid.

Be Inspired:

> *"The Lord said, 'If as one people speaking the same language they have begun to do this, then nothing they plan to do will be impossible for them.'"*
> **Genesis 11:6**

The story of the Tower of Babel, although it didn't end well, is a testament to the importance of planning and strategy. We have been created with the ability to accomplish our goals and make things happen, but only if we make a plan and stick to it.

Get Coached:

What hinders your productivity throughout the day? In what way will reviewing your agenda help you overcome that hindrance?

Take Action:

Print out your agenda for tomorrow and keep it with what you will be using tomorrow morning. Having a hard copy in front of you will allow you to make notes and commit it to your memory.

SUCCESS HABITS
VISUALIZATION AND CONFESSION

"The words of your mouth (your confessions) are powerful. They reflect what you believe, and what you believe shapes your life."
- Dr. Dave Martin, *The Force of Favor*

Daily Habit #11:
Visualizing and Confessing Success

There are very few things that carry as much weight as the words that you say. Once spoken, words cannot be altered or adjusted. They cannot be taken back or forgotten. Words are important. One of the companions of your words is what you visualize. What you expect to happen will quite often become reality.

Visualization and confession are the final elements of the investment in success portion of your morning routine. They are two sides of the same coin; what you believe will happen, or what you visualize, becomes what you say out loud, or what you confess. If you visualize and confess negativity, that's what you'll encounter in your day. If you visualize and confess positivity, productivity, and success, you will fill your day with such things. What you believe and what you say out loud have a direct impact on your success.

While visualization and confession are closely related, they are not the same thing. It is important to understand their differences so that you're able to implement these habits in your life. Here are a few tips to help you to adopt these habits.

Visualize

Look at the items on your agenda and visualize how you are going to accomplish them. Think of possible problems or issues that could arise in your efforts to complete each item and come up with resolutions to those problems. Preparation for those issues will eliminate hesitation should they actually arise.

Confess

In his book *The Force of Favor*, Dr. Dave Martin says confession is "a powerful act of faith that can activate the presence and promises of God in your life, because, if you say it loud enough and often enough, it will finally begin to seep into your heart and mind, affecting the way you think, the way you feel, the way you perceive the world, and the way you live your life."

It may sound silly, but encourage yourself! Speak words of life regarding your upcoming day. Confession is a biblical principle that allows us to be confronted with the power of our words. Saying what you will accomplish successfully aloud will bring your mind into alignment with your goals. You will get everything done; you will accomplish your goals.

Be Inspired:

> *"If we confess our sins, he is faithful and just and will forgive us our sins and purify us from all unrighteousness." 1*
> **John 1:9**

Confession not only has an impact on us, but it also moves the very heart of God! The power of confession is irrefutable. Something significant takes place when we practice confession.

Get Coached:

What are you visualizing and confessing about your life and your success? Are you cultivating positivity?

Take Action:

At the end of your investment in success routine, visualize your success and confess it with your mouth. Even if you feel silly, push through. Visualize your success and then say it out loud. Encourage yourself.

HEALTH HABITS

INVEST IN HEALTH

W e've discussed the importance of investing in your spiritual life and your success, now it's time to shift our focus. This is about more than just growing your mind, although that is definitely an important component; this is about investing in your health. Although this book is broken down into sections that address the various areas of life, our goal here is holistic growth. Your health is an important part of that journey.

The way you think about your body directly impacts your ability to invest in your physical health. If you believe that your health exists in a realm separate from your success and spiritual life, you will be unable to approach it appropriately. Everything in your life is connected; the way you treat your body has a direct impact on your ability to lead, succeed, and your reputation. Whether we like it or not, our health has a massive impact on the way we view ourselves and the way others view us. Truth be told, others judge us by our appearance. No one likes it, but it is the absolute truth.

It is critical to invest in your physical health when you are looking to grow. Why is health so important? Studies show that there is an undisputable link between physical activity, cognition, and executive control. Cognition refers to our ability to think and reason; executive control speaks to a division of goal oriented processes involved in our ability to perceive, remember, and act; specifically, executive control is about scheduling, planning, and multitasking. I don't know about you, but those things are pretty important in my professional and personal lives! Physical activity has a physiological effect on the way our brain processes and retains information. Being committed to your health quite literally makes you smarter and increases your capacity for excellence!

When it comes to your health, possessing the right mindset is a must. The goal is not to chase a number on a scale or have the stamina to run a certain number of miles; the goal is to be disciplined and a good steward of the body you have been given. This is the only body you will ever have and the only life you will ever live. Let me encourage you to do whatever you can to make sure you live this life well. You cannot live your best life until you invest in your physical health.

The turning point in my health journey came when I addressed the mental roadblocks that were hindering my success. I had to conquer the psychological deterrents before I could make any progress. The way I handled this was to identify reasons why I wanted to be healthy; I chose three motivating factors and focused on them. When discouragement or weariness would come, I would remind myself of those three things, and they would give me the strength to push forward. Your health journey will change drastically when you get motivated to make progress. Once I overcame those mental roadblocks, I was able to implement these five simple habits.

HEALTH HABITS
GO FOR A WALK

"Exercise and application produce order in our affairs, health of body, cheerfulness of mind, and these make us precious to our friends."
- Thomas Jefferson, *The Family Letters of Thomas Jefferson*

Daily Habit #12: Get Active

This habit is crucial. Eating well can only take you so far; you have to get active. This can

sound daunting to someone who doesn't exercise regularly, but it doesn't have to be overwhelming. Getting active can mean anything, from taking a walk to joining a gym. The details will vary in the life of every person. The important thing is that you get active in whatever way works for you.

When it comes to personal development, there is a very real temptation to compartmentalize your life and areas of growth. Even this book is divided into sections based on different targeted areas of growth. But there is a crucial difference between organization and isolation.

If you want to grow, you must do so holistically. Your physical health is just as important as your spiritual life and career. You cannot succeed in one area of life while neglecting another.

Studies show that less than 5% of adults participate in at least 30 minutes of physical activity per day. Only five percent! That's pretty low. If you made a list of the benefits of exercise, it would be pretty extensive. Not only is exercise helpful in weight management, it can also boost your energy, improve your mood, and even help you sleep better! Both your body and your mind will function at a higher level if you exercise regularly.

Exercise is an act of discipline. When you commit yourself to getting active and investing in your health, there is both a physical and a mental change. Regardless of the manner in which you choose to get active, the important thing is to you commit yourself wholeheartedly. When you commit to making this a part of your morning routine, you remove many of the opportunities to miss your workout. The morning is a special time of your day that you set aside just for yourself. When you exercise in the morning, not only do you get it out of the way early, you invest in a holistic growth model.

Be Inspired:

"Do you not know that your bodies are temples of the Holy Spirit, who is in you, whom you have received from God? You are not your own; you were bought at a price. Therefore, honor God with your bodies." 1 Corinthians 6:19-20. Your body is a gift from God! We take care of our bodies for the same reason we steward our finances well and work hard at our jobs—so that we will be able to glorify God in every area of life. Caring for your body is an act of worship.

Get Coached:

In what ways do you think compartmentalizing your growth can be harmful? What are some ways you can counteract compartmentalization?

Take Action:

I would like to challenge you to go for a walk. Studies show that a 20-25 minute walk every day will add 7.5 years to your life. That's incredible! I don't know about you, but I want those seven years. Get active! Be holistic in your pursuit of growth.

HEALTH HABITS
PLAN YOUR MEALS

"Your diet is a bank account. Good food choices are good investments."
- **Bethenny Frankel,** *Naturally Thin*

Daily Habit #13:
Plan Your Meals for the Day

I firmly believe planning and preparation are the keys to success. We have all probably heard the saying, "If you fail to plan, you plan to fail." It's a bit of a cliché, but I believe this statement to be true, especially when we are talking about health. For so many people, getting healthy is challenging. If you want to conquer this challenge, you must prepare and plan for success.

As I said, preparation is paramount. Think about where you are in your morning routine. You have already reviewed your agenda for today, so you know the direction your day is headed. Knowing your agenda prior to planning out your meals is important. When you know what your day holds, you are able to find the healthiest options that will fit into your schedule. You don't need to plan your day around food; the goal here is to plan your meals around your day.

Deciding where and when you will eat also helps you avoid mindless eating throughout the day. Having a snack is a good thing, and planning out your meals allows you to find the ideal time for a midafternoon pick-me-up. Whether you're planning your meals around your work schedule or your workouts, the important thing is to plan.

Have you ever tried this? Planning meals can sound complicated, but it doesn't have to be. Using the spaces below, complete a meal plan. Of course, there will be times that you'll deviate from this plan, and that's okay. This plan can serve as a great foundation for your day.

Breakfast:

_____
_____
_____

Snack:

_____
_____
_____

Lunch:

_____
_____
_____

Snack:

_____

_____

_____

Dinner:

_____

_____

_____

Be Inspired:

"Plans fail for lack of **counsel**, *but with many advisers they succeed."*
Proverbs 15:22

You've got to make a plan! Do your research, be aware of what the day will hold, and move forward. Your success is directly related to your willingness to plan.

Get Coached:

What kinds of things prevent you from making healthy choices throughout your day? Do you think planning out your meals will help counteract those things?

Take Action:

Use the space above to plan your meals for the day. Take time to prepare for today.

HEALTH HABITS
RECORD WHAT YOU EAT

"I believe that the greatest gift you can give your family and the world is a healthy you."
- Joyce Meyer, *Eat the Cookie… Buy the Shoes*

Daily Habit #14:
Keep a Record of Your Diet and Exercise

When trying to improve in any area, it's important to be aware of your actions. If you want to do something better, you must first identify areas of weakness. This is especially true when you're looking to get healthy. Before making changes, you must be fully cognizant of your existing habits.

You already have eating habits. The goal of this chapter is to show you how to make small changes where needed. When you take the time in your morning routine to review what you ate yesterday, you're able to identify areas that need improvement. For example, when reviewing your food journal, you're able to identify times of the day you're inclined to snack. If you know that you're going to want a snack at 3pm, make sure you have a healthy snack on hand instead of relying on chips from the vending machine.

Even beyond identifying areas for improvement, recording what you eat and your exercise keeps you accountable. Knowing you'll have to answer to yourself for the things you're eating or the workout you're thinking about skipping, you'll think twice before making less than ideal choices.

There are so many reasons to record your eating and exercise throughout the day; two of these reasons are to identify areas of weakness and to be accountable to yourself for your actions.

Be Inspired:

"The seven years of abundance in Egypt came to an end, and the seven years of famine began, just as Joseph had said. There was famine in all the other lands, but in the whole land of Egypt there was food."
Genesis 41:53-55

Had they lost track of what they were eating and saving, Egypt would have been facing a crisis. We may not be facing a famine as Joseph was, but we should be just as meticulous in our planning and records. Record what you eat so you can remain aware and in control of your health.

Get Coached:

Do you think reviewing your eating and exercise habits will be beneficial? Why or why not?

Take Action:

Download an app that will help you log what you're eating and how much you're exercising today. Keep track of your health habits. Every day you do this will make it easier to do tomorrow.

HEALTH HABITS
GAINING A DEEPER UNDERSTANDING

"The groundwork of all happiness is health."
- Leigh Hunt, *Poetical Works*

Daily Habit #15:
Learn One New Thing about Nutrition

I really believe that your health journey begins in your mind. For this reason, I am asking you to commit yourself to learn something new regarding physical health every day. When you understand more about your body and what it needs, it will be that much easier to pursue health. It is nearly impossible to grow in an area about which you know very little. As you learn more about nutrition, you will be better equipped to make progress on your health journey.

The reality is physical health is one of the most difficult areas for many people to master. Maybe you're one of those people who has never struggled with your health; if so, I applaud you! You are the kind of person the rest of the world envies. If you're like me, however, and your health is a challenging part of your life, I cannot explain to you the importance of deepening your understanding of health and nutrition. There's a difference between being *thin* and being *healthy*; you will develop a greater understanding of that difference as you commit to learning and growth in this area.

For many years, I knew all the tips and tricks to losing weight, but I was never able to lose weight and keep it off. Change only came as I discovered being healthy was more important than being thin. Investing in your physical health really isn't about losing weight; it is about discipline and stewardship. The best way to be disciplined and a good steward of your body is to continually expand your knowledge and understanding about nutrition and health.

There are many things you can do to implement this habit into your routine. Find a virtual mentor whose focus is on health; subscribe to a blog or purchase a book that will enlighten you and broaden your understanding of what it means to live a healthy life. You won't become an expert in nutrition overnight, but you can get a little better every day. Make it a priority to pursue understanding; health begins in your mind long before the results manifest in your body.

Be Inspired:

"For lack of guidance a nation falls, but victory is won through many advisers."
Proverbs 11:14

It doesn't get much clearer than this! Success doesn't happen in a vacuum; you need the wisdom of others to accomplish your goals.

Get Coached:

In what ways will a virtual health mentor encourage and strengthen you as you pursue better health?

Take Action:

Take some time today to find a virtual health mentor. Sign up for at least one blog or website subscription that will help you invest in your health.

HEALTH HABITS
REST

"Exercise to stimulate, not to annihilate. The world wasn't formed in a day, and neither were we. Set small goals and build upon them."
- Lee Haney, *(attrib.)*

Daily Habit #16: Plan for Rest

You may be wondering how rest fits into your morning routine—that's a good question! I would like you to think of your morning as a daily check-in. These morning habits are opportunities to plan and prepare for the day ahead. The keys to getting enough rest are planning and preparation. When you live a full, busy life, getting enough rest can very quickly fall to the bottom of your priority list. Rest is important; part of your morning routine should be to plan and prepare for an appropriate amount of rest. Rest manifests itself in three different ways: sleep, Sabbath, and fun. To be truly well rested, each of these three components must be present. Take a moment to download our free rest resource at dukematlock. com/downloadresources before we move forward.

Sleep

According to the Centers for Disease Control and Prevention (CDC), adults need somewhere between seven and eight hours of sleep per night. This isn't new information... Most of us are aware that eight hours of sleep per night is ideal. Any more or less can lead to sluggishness and reduced productivity. While eight hours is ideal, 30% of adults report an average of only six hours of sleep per night. A lack of sleep can lead to a wide variety of issues, including diabetes, depression, obesity, even increased mortality, and a reduced quality of life and productivity.

No matter how you look at it, sleep is important. But even so, many adults are not getting the appropriate amount of sleep. There are many possible reasons for this, like our continual connection to technology and social media, as well as our busy work schedules. It's difficult to fall asleep when you're still receiving and responding to work emails in bed. Sleep is huge; when you are well rested, you perform better, your mood improves, and you are able to tackle the items on your agenda. If you struggle getting enough sleep, I would encourage you to establish an end time for your day. By doing this, work becomes less of a hindrance to getting rest. Just as you end your work day, choose a time to turn off the television, put down your phone, and get into bed.

Mornings are the best time to choose a bedtime because your agenda is in front of you. You know what needs to get done and you also know that you need to get your eight hours of sleep. Plan out your day in a way that will allow you to accomplish your goals in enough time to get some rest.

Sabbath

In case you're unfamiliar with the term, a Sabbath day is a day of rest. The Sabbath is a Biblical concept that comes from God's creation of the world. Genesis 2:2-3 says, *"By the seventh day God had finished the work he had been doing; so on the seventh day he rested from all his work. Then God blessed the seventh day and made it holy, because on it he rested from all the work of creating that he had done."* The Sabbath became a mandate for the Jews. Honoring the Sabbath day and keeping it holy is even one of the Ten Commandments, meaning rest is just as important as being honest, abstaining from committing adultery, and not killing anyone!

The Sabbath is incredibly important in the Biblical narrative as well as in our lives today. We all know how important it is to work and to do so with excellence; the fact that you are even reading this book proves you are looking for avenues of growth and development. Becoming a better version of yourself and living with intention is hard work. But just as you do not shy away from working, you must not forget to give yourself a day off as well. You were not created to be in constant motion; the need to rest is present in every person.

A day of rest is impossible if your to-do list is never ending. If you feel as though you have too much to do, achieving those goals will become the priority. This is where the planning and preparation come into play. Choose your Sabbath, and then plan your week around that day.

Fun

The final component of being truly rested is fun. Just like sleep and your Sabbath, fun has to be planned and prepared for! Fun may look different for each person, but the details are not important. Fun may mean taking your kids to a park, going on vacation, or taking a day trip with friends. The important thing is to do something outside of your typical routine that you enjoy.

When you plan for fun, you break up the monotony of life. You have something to look forward to, something to reward yourself for all of your hard work. Doing something fun is absolutely necessary in your growth journey. Sometimes all you really need is to take a break and do something you enjoy. Having fun can reset your perspective and remind you how good life really is. Nothing fosters growth quite like a fresh perspective.

For me, going on vacation with my family has always been a priority. Once a year, my wife and I take our daughters on a trip, usually to the beach. These trips are not only refreshing—they are bonding experiences for our family, time when memories are made. Having fun on these trips, even in the most difficult seasons of our lives, brought my family closer together and reminded us just how blessed we were. I wouldn't trade those trips for anything, but they wouldn't have been possible if I hadn't planned for them.

Your health, relationships, and success all depend on your rest. It can seem counterproductive to stop working and rest, especially when you feel like you're building momentum. But no matter how much progress you are making, those victories will be short lived if you are not resting.

Be Inspired:

> "Remember the Sabbath day by keeping it holy. Six days you shall labor and do all your work, but the seventh day is a Sabbath to the Lord your God. On it you shall not do any work, neither you, nor your son or daughter, nor your male or female servant, nor your animals, nor any foreigner residing in your towns. For in six days the Lord made the heavens and the earth, the sea, and all that is in them, but he rested on the seventh day. Therefore, the Lord blessed the Sabbath day and made it holy."
> **Exodus 20:8-11**

Get Coached:

Where does rest fall on your list of priorities?

Take Action:

Get some sleep, choose a Sabbath day, and plan for fun! Invest in rest.

HABITS OF MARGIN

INVEST IN MARGIN

Margin is the framework of your life. It's the extra space, the reserves, or the wiggle room. Having margin in your finances means you're not facing a crisis when your washing machine breaks because you have reserves for emergencies. Margin in your personal and professional life means that you're balanced and well rounded, investing in success and personal relationships in a way that removes any competition between the two.

Let's face it, life is busy! There are always projects pending and people who need your attention. The daily demands of life can often leave us feeling as though there just aren't enough hours in the day. Dropping the ball on responsibilities isn't the best way to handle this kind of tension; but unfortunately, that's usually what happens. When something has got to give, it's usually your personal life that feels the loss. After all, when you have to choose between losing your job and losing sleep, sleep is usually the thing to go. But I would argue that instead of choosing between your responsibilities and your health, you need to create extra space in your life to handle the things that come up. Creating margin means you are building extra time into your schedule for the unexpected.

My grandmother had these really ornate bookends on her shelves; my mom had some as well. As a child, I loved those bookends. They were big, they looked cool, and they kept everything in place. As an adult, I love the concept of bookends. They're an endpoint, making it very clear that the books have stopped. If you want to create margin in your life, you have to bookend your day. Is it clear where your work stops and your personal life begins? For many of us, that distinction has yet to be made. We take work home, we sacrifice rest, and our families are put on the backburner… all because we simply don't have time to accomplish it all.

My days are filled with listening to and talking with people who love their work. They are committed, driven, and ambitious, but often something is hindering their success. I have also noticed that so many people in this position lack margin in their life. There are a few ways to tell if you're lacking margin in your life. Take a moment to read over the list below.

- The job seems to get bigger and more demanding every day.
- There always seems to be more on my plate than time in the day.
- When I go home, my mind is constantly racing with the things I still need to do at work.
- I often find myself staying at the office much later than I'm supposed to in an effort to get everything done.

If one or more of these things were descriptive of you, you're definitely dealing with a lack of margin. While this isn't ideal, there are simple ways to correct the issue. One of the easiest ways to do so is choosing a time for your work day to end. Ending your workday is critical; when you don't end your workday, you eliminate any opportunity for rest.

Bookending your day means choosing an end point. Decide what time you'll leave the office and head home. Then, take the last 15 minutes of your day to answer four questions, which we will discuss in the following four chapters. Bookending your day is all about giving yourself the space to rest and tackle your to-do list when you head into work the next day. You clear your mind, hold yourself accountable, and set the stage for productivity. Bookending your day really does make all the difference.

Bookending is about more than just your professional life; bookending is really about your family, your sleep, and your state of mind. It's hard going home and being present with your family or getting any rest when your mind is still at work. Ending your day and going home creates margin and space for things in your life other than your job. Bookend your day. Give yourself your best shot at success.

Before we move forward, take a minute to download the Bookend Your Day infograph at dukematlock.com/downloadresources. This will make it that much easier to follow along and implement these habits.

HABITS OF MARGIN
CELEBRATE YOUR DAY

*"The best preparation for tomorrow
is doing your best today."*
- H. Jackson Brown, Jr., *P.S. I Love You*

Daily Habit #17: Ask Yourself, "What Did I Get Done Today?"

As we just learned, bookending your day is an exercise in accountability and creating margin. In order to do this, you must buy into the process of choosing an end point for your work day. We are focusing on the final 15 minutes of your day to reflect on your accomplishments and what remains to be done tomorrow. There are four questions to answer in those last 15 minutes—the first of which being, "What did I get done today?"

Answering this question gives you a chance to review and celebrate. When you answer this question, I would recommend you pull out that day's agenda. Look at the list of things that you should have gotten done today. Having your agenda in front of you will be important as you work through answering this question.

Review your agenda. Read over today's goals. Which of those goals were accomplished? Be sure to physically check off or cross out what you can now take off your list for tomorrow. Crossing things off your list is a satisfying feeling! This is really an opportunity to celebrate your wins. Sometimes a long or difficult day can make you feel like you weren't able to accomplish much. When you answer this question, however, you confront reality instead of only your perception. Honesty is incredibly important when you are answering this question. Even if you only accomplished one thing, be honest about that and then celebrate the fact that you have one less thing to put on tomorrow's agenda.

Allow me to encourage you to get the most out of this exercise by writing out the answers to each of the four questions. When reviewing what you accomplished today, write out each item; write them out in detail and with intentionality. There are several reasons for this, one of which is to have a record of your work and accomplished goals. Another reason is to start seeing patterns in your work habits. To grow, you must first know yourself. Self-awareness precedes improvement and development.

Write out your answers, be honest with yourself, and be proud of what you've accomplished today! Allow yourself to be encouraged when you cross things off of your list. You've worked hard all day—celebrate those wins!

Be Inspired:

"At the dedication of the wall of Jerusalem, the Levites were sought out from where they lived and were brought to Jerusalem to celebrate joyfully the dedication with songs of thanksgiving and with the music of cymbals, harps and lyres."
Nehemiah 12:27

Take some time to celebrate! Just as the Israelites celebrated their hard work with a party, you should celebrate your accomplishments as well. You've tackled your projects and made progress, so be sure to acknowledge that.

Get Coached:

What did you get done today?

Take Action:

Bookend your day. Take time to reflect and celebrate the things you accomplished today.

HABITS OF MARGIN
EVALUATE YOUR DAY

"We must discipline ourselves to convert dreams into plans, and plans into goals, and goals into those small daily activities that will lead us, one sure step at a time, toward a better future."

- Jim Rohn, *Five Major Pieces to the Life Puzzle*

Daily Habit #18:
Ask Yourself, "What Did I Not Get Done Today?"

After you have identified what has been accomplished today, you must then move on to what was neglected. What you were unable to address today is just as important as what you were able to accomplish. Again, have your agenda for today on hand, as well as a place to write out a detailed answer to this question.

When looking back on your day and identifying what remains on the agenda, do so impartially. In other words, this step in the process of bookending your day is not meant to bring about negativity. Not getting something done does not mean that you've failed, it simply means that it remains on your list. Identifying those things will allow you to review your day and discover any patterns that are developing in your work habits. This is not meant to be an adverse experience, although it can be uncomfortable.

We don't answer this question to undo the mistakes that may have been made, or beat ourselves up for not achieving all of the day's goals. The reason we answer this question is to prepare for tomorrow. The best piece of advice I have ever received was to get a little better every day. You cannot, under any circumstances, get better if you aren't taking the time to reflect. When you reflect over the items on your agenda that did not get done, you give yourself the chance to come up with a game plan for tomorrow. If you want to accomplish something, you first have to identify the goal.

Once you have identified the items you were unable to accomplish today, look for patterns. Are all the things you didn't get done today related to a certain aspect of your job? It is common for a person with a more creative and innovative mind to fall behind on responding to emails or filling out paperwork for that day, simply because he was drawn to the areas of his job that he enjoys most.

Although it's common to give more attention to the tasks we enjoy most, this can hinder our overall productivity. If you want to figure out what parts of your job you're giving precedence to, you have to look for patterns in what is not getting done. To overcome this kind of a hindrance, you have to first identify it.

Be Inspired:

"Whatever you do, work heartily, as for the Lord and not for men..."
Colossians 3:23

Being diligent and hardworking doesn't free you from days in which some things don't get done. It happens. But be sure to apply that same diligence to bookending your day. Use this time to set the stage for tomorrow's productivity.

Get Coached:

What patterns arise in your working habits? What distracts you during the day?

Take Action:

Ask yourself, "What did I not get done today?" Make sure you write out your answer.

HABITS OF MARGIN
BE ACCOUNTABLE

*"By prevailing over all obstacles and distractions,
one may unfailingly arrive at his chosen goal or
destination."*
- Christopher Columbus, *(attrib.)*

Daily Habit #19:
Ask Yourself, "Why Did It Not Get Done?"

Once you've identified what items on your agenda didn't get done, you then need to understand why. Discovering why you were unable to accomplish your goals for the day is the only way to avoid repeating the action tomorrow. Just like you did when you answered the first two questions, make sure you have the day's agenda out and a place to write down the answers to these questions. Accountability is important. Only when you discover what exactly is hindering your productivity will you be able to find a solution.

The whole point of answering this question is to uncover the underlying problems. There are many reasons why things may not get finished during your work day. Some reasons are normal, like dealing with the unexpected or simply running out of time. Other reasons are not so normal, like taking a long lunch or spending too much time reading articles online. Regardless of the reason, you can alleviate a lack of productivity with proper planning. But before you can plan for tomorrow, you have to reflect on today.

My youngest daughter is an avid reader. When she was a little girl, she would carry books with her everywhere she went. She would even take them to the movie theater and read before the lights were turned down and the film started. She was teased relentlessly by her older sisters, of course, but it didn't deter her. She still carried her books with her. She is still, to this day, an avid reader. While in high school and college, however, she would read instead of doing homework. She would read when she should have been working, then run out of time to do her assignments. Something that was a good habit in her life became detrimental to her productivity when practiced at the wrong time.

Regardless of the distraction, even if it's reading or something beneficial to you in your life, if it's done at the wrong time, it's no longer a good thing. The right thing at the wrong time is the wrong thing.

Distractions and interruptions are a part of life. Stuff comes up and that's okay, but distractions and interruptions shouldn't become the norm. The problem could be too many items on your agenda. Or perhaps you are struggling to utilize your time properly. Whatever the case may be, spend time discovering what is hindering you from getting your work done.

Be Inspired:

"If you are wise, you are wise for yourself..."
Proverbs 9:12

Sometimes we have to hold ourselves accountable. The things you did and did not accomplish today are both your responsibility. Take this time to be honest with yourself about the wisdom you may or may not have exercised today. If you can't be honest with yourself about these things, you won't be able to be honest with anyone else about them.

Get Coached:

How often is your agenda derailed by distractions and interruptions? Why do you think that is?

Take Action:

Ask yourself, "Why did the items on my agenda not get done today?" Write out your answer.

HABITS OF MARGIN
PLAN FOR TOMORROW

"Always do your best. What you plant now, you will harvest later."
- Og Mandino, *The Greatest Salesman in the World*

Daily Habit #20: Ask Yourself, "What Am I Going to Get Done Tomorrow?"

This is probably the most important step of bookending your day. The steps up until this point were reflections on the past, while this step is all about planning for the future. Bottom line, even bookending your day doesn't grant you the ability to turn back the clock and change what was or was not accomplished today. All you have is the possibility of a productive tomorrow. Which, when you think about it, is a very hopeful thing.

When making your agenda for tomorrow, there are a few things you need to remember. The first is that when planning your day, you only want to plan about 85% of it. The remaining 15% you will want to leave open for the interruptions of life. Unexpected situations are bound to arise; it's just a part of life.

When you have 15% of your day set aside for interruptions or unexpected projects, those interruptions are much easier to deal with. Bookending your day is really about giving yourself your best shot at a full, productive tomorrow… so set aside that 15%. Interruptions will only ruin your ability to accomplish all of your tasks if you give them the power to do so.

Another thing you should pay attention to while building tomorrow's agenda is the number of items on your list. Shoot to have no more than seven and no less than five items on your agenda. Any less than five probably won't fill your workday and more than seven is probably too much to accomplish. Remember, the whole point of putting things on your to-do list is to do them! This isn't a long term plan; these are just your goals for tomorrow. Choose your goals well and be realistic about how long they will take to accomplish.

Bookending your day is an incredibly powerful process to create margin and optimize productivity. Building your agenda for tomorrow is the final step. Once you've listed 5–7 tasks you're going to get done tomorrow, put your agenda away. Go home, be with your family, and relax. Leave tomorrow's work for tomorrow. You will use your agenda tomorrow morning before you go to work, but don't need it until then. Give yourself some time to rest.

Be Inspired:

"Therefore do not worry about tomorrow, for tomorrow will worry about itself. Each day has enough trouble of its own."
Matthew 6:34

You can't tackle tomorrow's challenges today. There will be plenty of time to work and get things done tomorrow, so leave your agenda alone until then. You'll be more productive tomorrow if you allow yourself to rest and invest in your family today.

Get Coached:

How do you think leaving your agenda alone and going home will affect both your work and your relationships?

Take Action:

Ask yourself, "What am I going to get done tomorrow?" Make your agenda for tomorrow. Plan out 85% of the day and choose between five and seven items to put on your list.

INVEST IN YOURSELF
CREATE YOUR OWN HABIT

"We are what we repeatedly do. Excellence, then, is not an act, but a habit."
- Will Durant, *The Story of Philosophy*

Daily Habit #21:
Develop a Habit of Your Own That Will Help You Grow!

Recently, my daughter gave me *21 Seconds to Change Your World* by Dr. Mark Rutland. I was so moved by the content of the book that I added a new habit to my life. I now pray the Lord's Prayer during my morning routine. Although prayer and reading the Word were both established habits in my life, it wasn't until I read *21 Seconds* that I added the habit of focused prayer. The addition of the Lord's Prayer has added incredible value to my morning.

No one knows what you need quite like you do. You know your strengths and weaknesses; you know the areas in which you need to improve. The habits laid out in the preceding chapters are universal... anyone and everyone who implements them will experience growth. You may adjust these habits to suit you and your needs, but the habits themselves will remain the same. Having a foundation of healthy habits in your life is a powerful thing. I would encourage you to continue to build upon that foundation in your own way. This morning routine is a starting point, a launching pad from which you can start your day. It is not, however, the end of your growth journey.

So what are the areas in your life that could use improvement? Maybe you need to be more encouraging; maybe you need to be more intentional about the way you speak to your spouse or your children. I don't know what you need, but you do.

Once the areas of improvement are identified, spend some time thinking about developing a habit of your own, customized to help you accomplish that goal. For example, if you're looking to become more encouraging, you could develop the habit of writing thank you notes to those around you. It doesn't have to be a massive change; remember, these habits should be small, incremental changes.

Be Inspired:

> *"As water reflects the face, so one's life reflects the heart."*
> **Proverbs 27:19**

The way you live your life is a direct reflection of the state of your heart. Perfection is unattainable. You will never be perfect or be able to completely avoid making mistakes. The goal is not perfection, but continual growth. When you spend your time developing new habits and getting a little bit better every day, your life will become a reflection of a heart dedicated to pleasing God in every area of life.

Get Coached:

What habit can you implement today that will help you grow in weak areas?

Take Action:

If you haven't done so already, go back and reflect on the areas of your life that need improvement. What are those areas? What practical steps can you take to translate new habits into growth and improvement? Come up with a game plan for how you want to deal with these areas in your life.

CONCLUSION

Well, here we are friends. I hope you're singing Shania Twain's "Looks Like We Made It" because I sure am. A strong morning routine is the key to success and I truly believe the implementation of these 21 Habits will change your life. Private discipline precedes public victory every time.

I am so grateful that you came on this journey with me. I cannot wait for you to experience the kind of growth and development that I experienced when I began adopting these habits. The way you spend your morning matters. Use that time to invest in yourself and invest in success.

Below, you will find a summary of each of the 21 Habits we've discussed. I would encourage you to use this list every morning to ensure that you've accomplished each of these objectives. It will take time for this routine to become second nature for you. Until it does, read over these habits daily.

1. **Take Advantage of the Morning.** The morning is one of the most significant times of the day. When you

own your morning, you are able to create time in your schedule to invest in yourself.

2. **Have a Virtual Spiritual Mentor.** It's of vital importance that you allow others to invest in you spiritually, so be sure to find a virtual mentor. Because my morning is on a tight schedule, I need the investment from my mentor to be quick and concise.

3. **Daily Reading Plan.** The second step in my spiritual investment routine is to read my Bible. Having a reading plan helps me stay accountable and focused in my reading. The important thing is to stick to it.

4. **Read One Chapter of a Book.** Be sure to choose a book that is focused on spiritual growth and development. Regardless of the book chosen, you want to make sure you're reading at least 10 pages or one chapter per day.

5. **Reflect and Pray.** You've heard from others, you've read your Bible, and now it's time to reflect on what you're learning. Be sure to remember that although the voices of other people are important and beneficial, they don't outweigh the voice of God. Give yourself room to talk to God.

6. **Journal.** Journaling creates a record of what you're learning, gives you the opportunity to set spiritual goals, and records evidence of all your answered prayers down the line. You are doing a lot of different things in this time of investment, so make sure you bring everything together at the end. Journaling is the best way to do that.

7. **Have a Virtual Success Mentor.** Once you've closed your journal, it's time to shift gears from spirituality to success. Watching or reading something from your virtual mentor is a great way to do that.

8. **Daily Gratitude.** This portion of your morning is vitally important. When you spend time reflecting on things that you're grateful for, you renew your mind and combat negativity. A grateful mind is a successful one.

9. **Read.** Choose a book that's written about leadership or success. I've heard it said that you can finish school, but you should never end your education. Use this time to grow your mind and learn about your field. Be sure to read at least ten pages or one chapter per day.

10. **Review your agenda.** Remember when we talked about bookending your day? Part of that process is creating an agenda for the next day, and now it's time to pull that agenda back out. Review the items on your list and familiarize yourself with it again.

11. **Visualization and Confession.** Look at the items on your agenda and visualize how you're going to accomplish them. Speak words of life regarding your upcoming day. Saying what you'll accomplish successfully aloud will bring your mind into alignment with your goals.

12. **Go for a Walk.** This walk in the morning has become my favorite part of the day. On my blog, I wrote about my morning walk routine, so be sure to check that post

out for more information. Regardless of what activity you choose to do, it's important that you do something.

13. **Plan Out Meals for the Day.** You know what your day is going to look like, so now you can plan what you're going to eat and how to find the healthiest options that will fit into your schedule. This will also help eliminate mindless eating throughout the day.

14. **Record What You Eat.** I use MyFitnessPal, which is an app that allows me to log my eating and track my calorie intake. This app is free and I'd highly recommend it to anyone looking to become more disciplined or even just more aware of their eating habits.

15. **Learn One New Thing About Nutrition.** Your awareness and ability to be healthy will increase as your knowledge increases. Grow your mind as you discipline your body.

16. **Rest.** You cannot be a whole, healthy person if you don't allow yourself to rest. Remember to rest in three ways: sleep, Sabbath, and fun.

17. **Ask, "What did I get done today?"** This is a moment to celebrate your accomplishments. You worked hard all day, so be sure to acknowledge and celebrate what you were able to get done.

18. **Ask, "What did I not get done today?"** This is an important moment because you have the chance to identify the specific things that remain on your agenda. Take this opportunity to prioritize and assess your upcoming responsibilities.

19. **Ask, "Why did it not get done?"** Accountability is important. Be honest with yourself. Did you just run out of time? Did you take a long lunch or spend too much time reading Buzzfeed articles? Figure out what happened so it doesn't happen again tomorrow

20. **Ask, "What's next?"** Make a new agenda for tomorrow. This is an exercise in accountability. Write out your agenda and then leave it alone until tomorrow.

21. **Develop Your Own Habit.** Assess your strengths and weaknesses. Identify an area in which you would like to grow and implement a habit that will lead to improvement.

ABOUT THE AUTHOR

Duke Matlock is a speaker, coach, and consultant. He is the founder of Invest Leadership Initiative, where he helps leaders facing personal and organizational challenges develop and grow by investing in themselves, assuring the realization of success and life fulfillment.

END NOTES

1. http://www.isbe.net/epe/pdf/reports-webinars/iphi-epetf-rpt0313.pdf
2. http://www.fitness.gov/resource-center/facts-and-statistics/
3. http://www.mayoclinic.org/healthy-lifestyle/fitness/in-depth/exercise/art-20048389?pg=2
4. http://www.cdc.gov/features/dssleep/
5. medpagetoday.com/meetingcoverage/apss/9772
6. Storey, T. (2010). *Comeback & beyond*. Tulsa, OK: Harrison House.
7. Martin, D. (2001). *The force of favor*. Favor International.

WHAT IS A GROWTH COACH?

There are a few ways you can tap into your potential and exploit yourself as your greatest resource. The first is to invest in a coaching relationship. Implementing healthy habits in your life is a guaranteed way to experience growth. But there is another way to invest in yourself, and that is by investing in a coaching relationship. It's not a coach's job to tell you what to do or come up with their own strategy for your personal growth; a coach's job is to ask you questions and create awareness... both of which help you develop a new perspective.

My favorite way to describe a coach is through the imagery of a boxing match. In the ring, there are only two people—the fighters. But if you watch closely, the boxers head back to their corners between each round. It's in these corners that they meet up with their "corner man," the guy holding the towels and water bottle, gluing the boxer's eye closed between rounds. Moments spent in the corner give boxers the strength to keep on fighting; because where the boxer can only see what is directly in front of him, the corner man can see the whole picture. The corner man sees things the fighter is unable to see. The best fighter in the world could not win a fight without his corner man.

A coach is a person in your corner. A coach's job is to stand behind you and support you, helping you accomplish your goals and win the fight. A coach is your resource in the trenches; no matter what you're facing, your coach's job is to help you gain a new perspective and achieve your goals. A coach is committed to your success.

We have a team ready to help you go to the next level. If you are interested in investing in a coaching relationship, head to dukematlock.com for more information.

If you would like to get the most out of *Get Up and Grow: 21 Habits of Successful People*, you need to invest in a coaching relationship. This coaching package will connect you with a coach who will walk you through the Get Up and Grow process, allowing you to make the most of your mornings and work towards exponential growth.

Visit the link to the left to invest in yourself and guarantee your success! dukematlock.com/get-upcoaching

MINISTERS MASTERMIND

A community for highly motivatedPastors to expand their leadership capacity, share ideas, and build relationships, while be challenged and encouraged!

VISIT
DUKEMATLOCK.COM/MINISTERSMASTERMIND
FOR MORE INFO!

COMING SOON!

GROWTH UNIVERSITY

Growth University is a community for leaders looking to grow exponentially. Courses, leadership mentors, and book reviews are just a few examples of all this group has to offer!

WATCH
DUKEMATLOCK.COM
FOR FUTURE UPDATES!

@DUKEMATLOCK

 FACEBOOK.COM/DUKEMATLOCK

 INSTAGRAM.COM/DUKEMATLOCK

 LINKEDIN.COM/IN/DUKEMATLOCK1

 PINTEREST.COM/DUKEMATLOCK

The best way to guarantee continued growth and ongoing
development is to subscribe to my blog. Weekly posts focused
on personal and professional development, investing in
yourself and success, and leadership will help you cultivate
a culture of growth in your life. Subscribe today and
stay up to date on everything that is happening
at Invest Leadership Initiative.

DUKEMATLOCK.COM

Morgan James
Speakers Group

We connect Morgan James published
authors with live and online events
and audiences who will benefit
from their expertise.

Printed in the USA
CPSIA information can be obtained
at www.ICGtesting.com
JSHW082358140824
68134JS00020B/2153